A PLUME BOOK
101 WAYS TO KILL YOUR BOSS

GRAHAM ROUMIEU is a nonhomicidal author and illustrator from Canada. You might also enjoy some of his other less violent books (but still with some good violent bits), *Bigfoot: I Not Dead*, *Me Write Book: It Bigfoot Memoir*, and *In Me Own Words: The Autobiography of Bigfoot*.

ALSO BY GRAHAM ROUMIEU

In Me Own Words
Me Write Book
Cat and Gnome

101 WAYS TO KILL YOUR BOSS
Graham Roumieu

A PLUME BOOK

PLUME
Published by the Penguin Group
Penguin Group (USA) Inc., 375 Hudson Street, New York, New York 10014, U.S.A.
Penguin Group (Canada), 90 Eglinton Avenue East, Suite 700, Toronto, Ontario, Canada M4P 2Y3
(a division of Pearson Penguin Canada Inc.)
Penguin Books Ltd., 80 Strand, London WC2R 0RL, England
Penguin Ireland, 25 St. Stephen's Green, Dublin 2, Ireland (a division of Penguin Books Ltd.)
Penguin Group (Australia), 250 Camberwell Road, Camberwell, Victoria 3124, Australia (a division of Pearson Australia Group Pty. Ltd.)
Penguin Books India Pvt. Ltd., 11 Community Centre, Panchsheel Park, New Delhi – 110 017, India
Penguin Group (NZ), 67 Apollo Drive, Rosedale, North Shore 0632, New Zealand (a division of Pearson New Zealand Ltd)
Penguin Books (South Africa) (Pty.) Ltd., 24 Sturdee Avenue, Rosebank, Johannesburg 2196, South Africa

Penguin Books Ltd., Registered Offices: 80 Strand, London WC2R 0RL, England

First published by Plume, a member of Penguin Group (USA) Inc.

First Printing, January 2009
10 9 8 7 6 5 4 3 2 1

Ⓟ REGISTERED TRADEMARK—MARCA REGISTRADA

CIP data is available.
ISBN 978-0-452-29005-1

Printed in the United States of America

BOOKS ARE AVAILABLE AT QUANTITY DISCOUNTS WHEN USED TO PROMOTE PRODUCTS OR SERVICES. FOR INFORMATION PLEASE WRITE TO PREMIUM MARKETING DIVISION, PENGUIN GROUP (USA) INC., 375 HUDSON STREET, NEW YORK, NEW YORK 10014.

For Dad

101 WAYS TO KILL YOUR BOSS

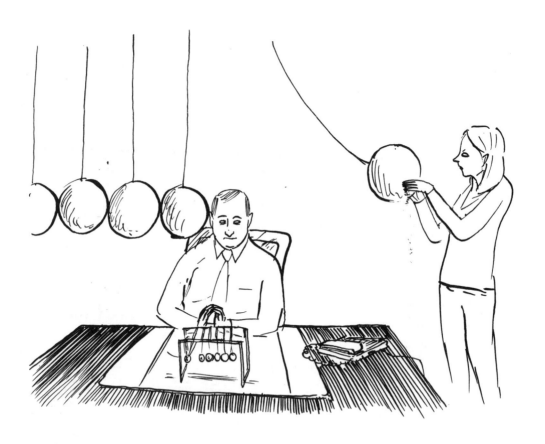

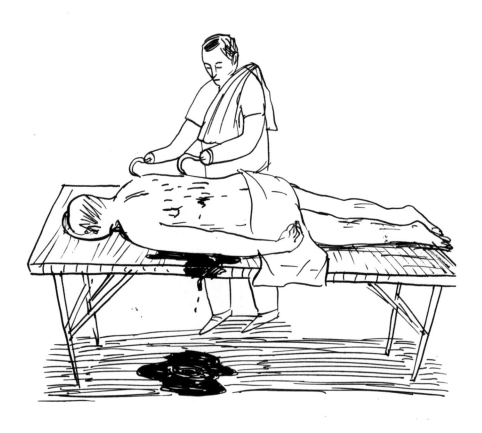

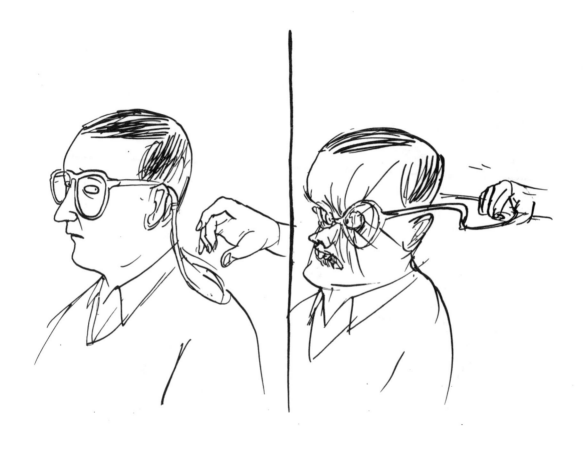

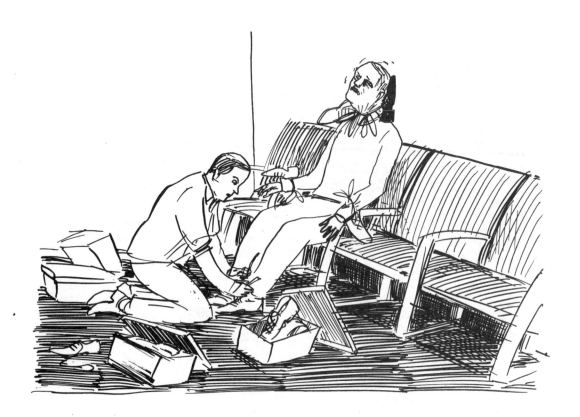

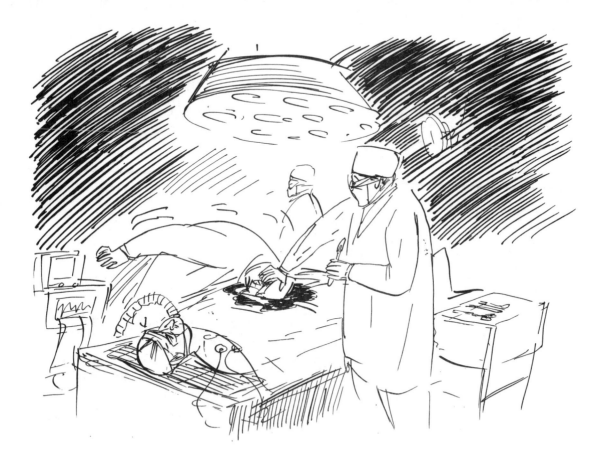

Graham Roumieu

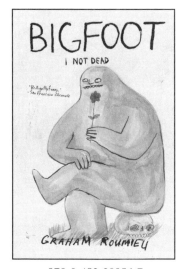

978-0-452-28956-7

"So freaking funny you'll be out of breath."
—Salon.com

978-0-452-28685-6

www.roumieu.com

Plume
A member of Penguin Group (USA) Inc.
www.penguin.com